# *Wood Pellet Smoker and Grill Cookbook*

## *Ultimate Smoker Cookbook for Real Barbecue, The Art of Smoking Meat for Real Pitmasters*

### *By Gary Mercer*

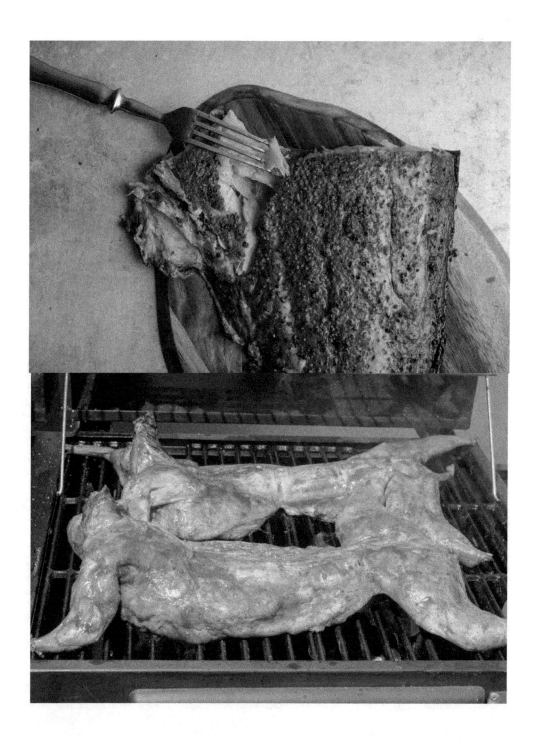

# TABLE OF CONTENTS

## Why Smoking ............................................................. 8

## Chapter-1 BEEF ........................................................ 10
- BEEF POT ROAST ............................................................. 10
- BOLOGNESE ..................................................................... 13
- CHILLI CON CARNE WITH DARK CHOCOLATE & COFFEE ................. 16
- RIBEYE STEAK .................................................................. 20
- SMOKED BEEF BURGER WITH WHISKEY SAUCE .......................... 22

## Chapter-2 CHICKEN & TURKEY ....................... 26
- ASIAN-STYLE TURKEY JERKY ............................................... 26
- BARBECUE SMOKED CHICKEN WINGS ................................... 29
- DEVILED EGGS .................................................................. 31
- ITALIAN CHICKEN PARMIGIANA .......................................... 33
- MESQUITE SMOKED CHICKEN ............................................. 35
- SMOKED TURKEY BURGERS ................................................ 38

## Chapter-3 LAMB ..................................................... 40
- LAMB BURGERS WITH CHEESE............................................. 40
- LAMB CHOPS WITH GARLIC & HERBS ................................... 43
- LAMB JERKY ..................................................................... 46
- SEASONED LEG OF LAM ..................................................... 48
- SMOKED LAMB SAUSAGE WITH YOGURT SAUCE ..................... 51

## Chapter-4 PORK .................................................................. 54

BISCUITS & SMOKED SAUSAGE GRAVY ............................................... 54
JALAPENO CHEDDAR SMOKED SAUSAGE ............................................ 58
PORK BUTT SANDWICH ............................................................................ 61
SMOKED APPLEWOOD BACON ................................................................. 64
ST LOUIS RIBS WITH COCONUT BBQ RIB SAUCE ............................... 67

## Chapter-5 FISH .................................................................... 70

FENNEL & PEPPER STUFFED SMOKED TROUT ..................................... 70
HERB SMOKED SALMON .......................................................................... 72
SESAME CRUSTED SMOKED HALIBUT WITH TAHINI MAYO ............ 75

## Chapter-6 SEAFOOD ......................................................... 78

HICKORY SMOKED CAJUN SHRIMP ....................................................... 78
LITTLENECK SMOKED CLAMS ................................................................. 81
PAPRIKA & GARLIC BUTTER SMOKED LOBSTER TAILS ..................... 83

## Chapter-7 GAME.................................................................. 86

BISON & BOAR SAUSAGES ........................................................................ 86
DUCK LEGS WITH POLENTA & MUSHROOMS ..................................... 89
SMOKED BBQ RABBIT ............................................................................... 93

## Chapter-8 VEGETABLES .................................................... 96

CAJUN ARTICHOKES .................................................................................. 96
SMOKED OLIVES ......................................................................................... 98
SMOKED VEGGIE MEDLEY ...................................................................... 100

## Chapter-9 Smoking Tips and Tricks ............... 102
Difference Between Barbequing and Smoking .............................. 102
Difference Between Cold And Hot Smoking .................................. 103
Basic Preparations ....................................................................... 104
Elements of Smoking .................................................................. 105
Choose your wood ...................................................................... 107
Select the right meat .................................................................. 110
Find the right temperature ......................................................... 111

## Conclusion ...................................................... 112

## Get Your FREE Gift ......................................... 113

## Other books by Gary Mercer ....................... 114

# WHY SMOKING

The ultimate how-to guide for smoking all types of meat, poultry, fish, vegetables and game. This book on smoking meats for beginners is the guide to mastering the low and slow art of smoking beef, fish, seafood, poultry, pork, vegetables, and game at your home. This guide is an essential book for beginners who want to smoke meat without needing expert help from others. This book offers detailed guidance obtained by years of smoking meat, includes clear instructions and step-by-step directions for every recipe. The book includes photographs of every finished meal to make your job easier. Whether you are a beginner meat smoker or looking to go beyond the basics, the book gives you the tools and tips you need to start that perfectly smoked meat.

Smoking is generally used as one of the cooking methods now days. The food enrich in protein such as meat would spoil quickly, if cooked for a longer period of time with modern cooking techniques. Whereas, Smoking is a low & slow process of cooking the meat. Where there is a smoke, there is a flavor. With white smoke, you can boost the flavor of your food. In addition to this statement, you can preserve the nutrition present inside the food as well. This is flexible & one of the oldest techniques of making food. It's essential for you to brush the marinade over your food while you cook and let the miracle happen. The only thing you need to do is to add a handful of fresh coals or wood chips as and when required. Just taste your regular grilled meat and a smoked meat, you yourself would find the difference. Remember one thing i.e. "Smoking is an art". With a little time & practice even you can become an expert. Once you become an expert with smoking technique, believe me you would never look for other cooking techniques. To find one which smoking technique works for you, you must experiment with different woods & cooking methods. Just cook the meat over indirect heat source & cook it for hours. When smoking your meats, it's very important that you let the smoke to escape & move around.

# CHAPTER-1 BEEF

# BEEF POT ROAST

## (TOTAL COOK TIME 5 HOURS 40 MINUTES)

**INGREDIENTS FOR 4 SERVINGS**

**THE MEAT**

- Chuck roast (2-lb, 0.9-kgs)

## THE RUB

- Garlic powder – 1 teaspoon
- Onion powder – 1 teaspoon
- Kosher salt – 1 teaspoon
- Black pepper – 1 teaspoon

## THE INGREDIENTS

- Red potatoes, halved – 2 cups
- Carrots, diced – 2 cups
- Pearl onions, peeled – 2 cups
- Ancho chili powder – 1 teaspoon
- Red wine – 1 cup
- Fresh rosemary – 1 tablespoon
- Fresh thyme – 1 tablespoon
- 2 dried chipotle pepper
- Chicken stock – 2 cups

## THE SMOKE

- When you are ready to beginning cooking, set your grill to smoke and with the lid closed, preheat for 12-15 minutes
- Maple wood pellets are a good choice for this recipe

# METHOD

1. In a bowl, combine the garlic powder with the onion powder, kosher salt, and black pepper and rub all over the chuck roast.
2. Smoke the meat for 90 minutes before removing from the smoker grill and increasing the temperature to 275°F (135°C).
3. Transfer the smoked roast along with the red potatoes, carrots, pearl onions, Ancho chili powder, red wine, rosemary, thyme, chipotle pepper and stock to a Dutch oven.
4. Cover the Dutch oven with a lid and place in the smoker. Braise for 4-5 hours, until the meat is tender.
5. Serve and enjoy.

# *BOLOGNESE*

## (TOTAL COOK TIME 1 HOUR 30 MINUTES)

## INGREDIENTS FOR 4 SERVINGS

## THE MEAT

- Ground beef (2-lbs, 0.9-kgs)

## THE INGREDIENTS

- Olive oil – 1 tablespoon
- 3 cloves of garlic, peeled, and minced
- 1 onion, peeled and chopped
- 3 large tomatoes, chopped
- Tomato sauce – 2 cups
- Paprika – 2 teaspoons
- Dried oregano – 2 teaspoons
- Dried basil – 1 teaspoon
- Spaghetti
- Butter – 1 tablespoon
- Parmesan cheese, freshly grated, to serve

## THE SMOKE

- When you are ready to beginning cooking, preheat the smoker to 225°F ( 107°C)
- Applewood pellets are a good choice for this recipe

# METHOD

1. First, heat the oil in a deep pan.
2. Add the beef followed by the garlic and onions to the pan.
3. Once the beef browns and the onions are translucent, add the tomatoes followed by the tomato sauce, paprika, oregano, basil, salt, and black pepper. Stir to combine.
4. Allow to simmer for 5 minutes, while occasionally stirring.
5. Remove the pan from the stove top and place in the smoker.
6. Smoke for between 1-1½ hours while occasionally stirring.
7. While the sauce smokes, cook the pasta until al dente.
8. Once the sauce is ready, remove it from the smoker and stir in the butter.
9. Once cooked, drain the pasta and serve with the sauce.
10. Sprinkle with grated Parmesan and enjoy.

# CHILLI CON CARNE WITH DARK CHOCOLATE & COFFEE

## (TOTAL COOK TIME 2 HOURS 5 MINUTES)

## INGREDIENTS FOR 6 SERVINGS

### THE MEAT

- Ground chuck (2-lbs, 0.9-kgs)

## THE INGREDIENTS

- Olive oil – 2 tablespoons
- 1 large onion, peeled and diced
- 1 red bell pepper, seeded and diced
- 3 garlic cloves, peeled and minced
- Kosher salt
- Tomato paste – 2 tablespoons
- Chili powder – 2 tablespoons
- Ground cumin – 1 tablespoon
- Dried oregano – 1 teaspoon
- Beef stock – 2 cups
- Strongly brewed coffee – ½ cup
- 2 cans chili beans and sauce (15-ozs, 425-gms) each
- 1 can diced tomatoes (15-ozs, 425-gms)
- Dark chocolate (2-ozs, 57-gms)

## THE EXTRAS

- Cilantro, chopped
- Cheese, grated
- Green onions, chopped
- Sour cream, store-bought

## THE SMOKE

- When you are ready to beginning cooking, set the smoker grill to 350°F (177°C) and with the lid closed, preheat for 12-15 minutes
- Place a Dutch oven on the grill grate
- Cherry wood pellets are a good choice for this recipe

## METHOD

1. Once the Dutch oven is sufficiently hot, and the smoker grill temperature has been reached, in the Dutch oven combine the olive oil with the onion, bell pepper, garlic and a pinch of salt. Close the lid, and while occasionally stirring cook for 10-12 minutes, or until the peppers and onions are softened.
2. Next, add the meat, and using the back of a wooden spoon break the meat up. Cover with the lid, and cook until nearly cooked through and crumbly; for an additional 8-10 minutes.
3. Stir in the tomato paste along with the chili powder, cumin, and oregano and cook until the meat is evenly coated, for a couple of minutes.
4. Pour in the stock, followed by the coffee and stir well to combine.
5. Close the lid and simmer the chili, stirring only once, for 10 minutes.
6. Add the chili beans, diced tomatoes, and dark chocolate and stir well.
7. Close the lid and simmer for 15-20 minutes, this will allow the chili to thicken.
8. Taste and season as necessary.

9. For added smokiness, turn the heat to smoke and leave the chili on the grill for up to 60 minutes.
10. Serve with chopped cilantro, grated cheese, chopped onions and a dollop of sour cream.

# *RIBEYE STEAK*

## (TOTAL COOK TIME 1 HOUR)

## INGREDIENTS FOR 1 SERVING

## THE MEAT

- 1 ribeye steak, 2-ins (5-cms) thick
- Steak rub, of choice

## THE SMOKE

- When you are ready to beginning cooking, preheat your grill to low smoke

## METHOD

1. Allow the ribeye to rest at room temperature for half an hour.
2. Season the steak with the steak rub.
3. Place the ribeye on the grill and allow to smoke for between 20-25 minutes.
4. Remove the steak from the grill and adjust the heat to 400°F (204°C).
5. Return the steak to the grill and sear on each side for 4-5 minutes.
6. Cook the steak to your preferred level of doneness.
7. Wrap in foil and allow to rest for several minutes before serving.

# SMOKED BEEF BURGER WITH WHISKEY SAUCE

## (TOTAL COOK TIME 1 HOUR 30 MINUTES)

**INGREDIENTS FOR 4 SERVINGS**

**THE MEAT**

- Ground sirloin (1-lb, 0.45-kgs)

## THE SAUCE

- 1 can pineapple rings plus juice (20-ozs, 567-gms)
- Vegetable oil – 1 tablespoon
- ¼ cup yellow onion, peeled and diced
- Kosher salt
- 3 garlic cloves, peeled and finely minced
- Whiskey – 3 tablespoons
- Brown sugar – 1 cup
- Ginger – 1 teaspoon
- Soy sauce – ½ cup
- Water – ⅓ cup
- Hot sauce – 1 teaspoon

## THE INGREDIENTS

- Whisky – 2 teaspoons
- Kosher salt
- Beef rub – 1 tablespoon
- 4 slices of Cheddar cheese
- 4 hamburger buns, split
- Pineapple, grilled
- Caramelized onion
- Bacon, cooked and crispy

## THE SMOKE

- When you are ready to beginning cooking, set your grill to smoke and preheat for 5-10 minutes
- Oak wood pellets are a good choice for this recipe

## METHOD

1. Strain the juice from the canned pineapples and set aside 1 cup for the sauce.
2. Put the pineapple rings aside, for grilling later.
3. For the sauce: In a pan over moderate heat, heat the oil.
4. Add the onions followed by a pinch of salt and cook while occasionally stirring for 5 minutes, or until the onions are softened, and translucent.
5. Add the garlic and cook for an additional 60 seconds.
6. Pour in the whiskey and burn the alcohol off for 30 seconds.
7. Whisk in the brown sugar together with the ginger followed by the pineapple juice, soy sauce, and water. Bring boil before reducing the heat and simmering until the sauce thickens and easily coats the back of a spoon, for approximately 10 minutes.
8. For the beef burgers: Pour the whiskey into the ground beef together with 1 tsp of salt and using clean hands, gently combine.
9. Divide the mixture into 4 equal-sized portions, and gently flatten to create 4 patties. Lightly season on both sides with beef rub.

10. When you are ready to begin cooking, arrange the patties on the preheated grill, secure the lid and smoke for between 25-30 minutes.
11. Take the burgers off the grill and increase the heat to 450°F (232°C). Close the lid and preheat the grill for 10-15 minutes.
12. Arrange the patties on the hottest part of the grill and cook for 4 minutes.
13. Flip the burgers over and brush with a liberal amount of whiskey glaze. Cook for 2-3 minutes, before topping with Cheddar cheese.
14. Place the burger buns directly on the grill grate and toast for 2-3 minutes, until the cheese entirely melts. Grill the pineapple rings.
15. When you are ready to serve, add a spoonful of whiskey glaze to the bottom of the buns, top with the burger, grilled pineapple rings and load with toppings.
16. Serve and enjoy.

# Chapter-2 Chicken & Turkey

# Asian-Style Turkey Jerky

**(TOTAL COOK TIME 10 HOURS 25 MINUTES)**

## INGREDIENTS FOR 10-12 SERVINGS

## THE POULTRY

- Turkey breast (2-lbs, 0.9-kgs)

## THE MARINADE

- Salt – ½ teaspoon
- Ground ginger – ½ teaspoon
- Black pepper – ½ teaspoon
- Sugar – ¼ cup
- Low sodium soy sauce – ½ cup
- Fresh ginger root, chopped – 1 tablespoon
- 1 large clove of garlic, peeled and minced

## THE SMOKE

- Preheat your smoker to 160°F (71°C)

## METHOD

1. Cut the turkey breast meat ¼-ins (0.64-cms) strips.
2. In a large resealable bag, combine the salt together with the ground ginger, black pepper, sugar, soy sauce, fresh ginger, and garlic; mix well to combine.
3. Add the turkey strips to the resealable bag, seal, and gently massage to evenly coat. Transfer to the refrigerator to marinade, for 24 hours.
4. The following day, take the turkey out of the marinade and in a single layer, arrange the strips on the racks.
5. Smoke at 160°F (71°C), until the jerky is dry rather than crisp.
6. Set the jerky aside to cool to room temperature.
7. Enjoy.

# *BARBECUE SMOKED CHICKEN WINGS*

## (TOTAL COOK TIME 8 HOURS 35 MINUTES)

## INGREDIENTS FOR 2-4 SERVINGS

### THE POULTRY

- 8 chicken wings, wing tips discarded

## THE SEASONING

- Salt and freshly ground black pepper
- BBQ sauce, store-bought

## THE SMOKE

- Preheat the smoker, for indirect cooking to 225°f (107°c)
- Cherry wood chips are a good choice for this recipe

## METHOD

1. Season the chicken wings with salt and freshly ground black pepper and marinade in the barbecue sauce overnight.
2. Remove the wings from the marinade, shaking off any excess marinade and place in the hot smoker.
3. Smoke the chicken wings until their internal temperature reaches 165°F (74°C). Baste the wings with extra barbecue sauce when they are nearly ready.
4. Set aside to rest for 10 minutes before serving with a dollop of sauce on the side.

# *DEVILED EGGS*

## (TOTAL COOK TIME 9 HOURS 10 MINUTES)

## INGREDIENTS FOR 4 SERVINGS

## THE POULTRY

- 4 large-size eggs

## THE FILLING

- Mustard – 1 tablespoon
- Mayonnaise – ¼ cup
- Pinch of nutmeg

## THE SMOKE

- Preheat your smoker to 225°F (107°C)

## METHOD

1. Steam the eggs for 20 minutes, and in cold water, set aside to cool for 60 minutes.
2. Peel the eggs, and place in the fridge for up to 24 hours.
3. Smoke the whole eggs for 35-40 minutes.
4. Meanwhile, in a bowl, combine the mustard with the mayonnaise.
5. Place the smoked eggs in the fridge, overnight.
6. Lengthwise, cut the eggs in half and scoop the yolks into a small bowl.
7. Stir the mustard-mayo mixture into the yolks and combine.
8. Scoop the mixture back into the whites and garnish with a pinch of nutmeg.

# *ITALIAN CHICKEN PARMIGIANA*

### (TOTAL COOK TIME 1 HOUR)

## INGREDIENTS FOR 6-8 SERVINGS

## THE MEAT

- Boneless chicken breast fillets (2-lbs, 0.9-kgs)

## THE INGREDIENTS

- 4 egg whites
- Water – 2 tablespoons
- Italian seasoned breadcrumbs, any brand – 4 tablespoons
- Parmesan cheese, freshly grated – 4 tablespoons
- Marinara sauce, store-bought – 2 cups
- Mozzarella cheese, shredded – 2 cups

## SMOKE

- For indirect cooking preheat your smoker grill to 400°F (205°C)

## METHOD

1. In a shallow dish whisk the egg whites with the water.
2. In another shallow dish, toss the seasoned breadcrumbs with the freshly grated Parmesan.
3. Dip each chicken fillets in the egg whites and then the Parmesan breadcrumbs.
4. Arrange the chicken, in a single layer in a pan and place on the cooking grid. Cook for 30 minutes.
5. Pour the marinara sauce over the breaded chicken.
6. Sprinkle the mozzarella evenly over each filet.
7. Cook for an additional 5 minutes until the cheese entirely melts and the chicken's juices run clear.
8. Serve and enjoy.

# *MESQUITE SMOKED CHICKEN*

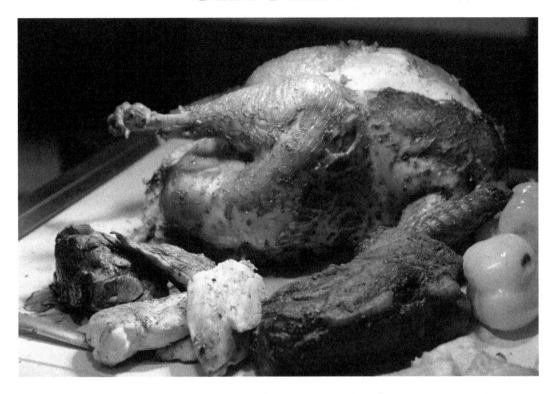

### (TOTAL COOK TIME 11 HOURS 45 MINUTES)

## INGREDIENTS FOR 6-8 SERVINGS

## THE POULTRY

- 1 whole chicken (3-lbs, 1.36-kgs)

## THE BRINE

- Kosher salt – ½ cup
- Brown sugar – 1 cup
- Water (1-gal, 3.8-lts)

## THE RUB

- 1 fresh lemon
- Onion, peeled and minced – 1 teaspoon
- 3 whole cloves of garlic, peeled
- 4 sprigs of thyme

## THE SMOKE

- Preheat your smoker with the lid open and establish the fire for between 4-5 minutes and preheat with the lid closed to 225°F (107°C)
- Mesquite wood chips are recommended for this recipe

## METHOD

1. First brine the chicken by dissolving the salt and the brown sugar in the water.
2. Add the chicken to the brine and transfer to the fridge, overnight. It is important that the bird is entirely submerged in the brine, so you may need to weigh it down.
3. While the grill preheats, remove the bird from the brine and using kitchen paper towel, pat dry.
4. Rub the chicken with the minced garlic and game rub.
5. Next, stuff the chicken cavity with lemon, onion, garlic, and thyme.
6. Using kitchen twine, tie the legs together.
7. Place the chicken directly on the grill grate and some for between 2½-3 hours or until an internal thermometer registers 160°F (71°C).
8. Set aside to rest, carve, and enjoy.

# *SMOKED TURKEY BURGERS*

**(TOTAL COOK TIME 30 MINUTES)**

## INGREDIENTS FOR 4-6 SERVINGS

## THE POULTRY

- Ground turkey (2-lbs, 0.9-gms)

## THE INGREDIENTS

- 6 green onions, thinly sliced
- Breadcrumbs – 1 cup
- Barbecue sauce, store-bought, of choice – ½ cup
- Ground oregano – 1 teaspoon
- Garlic powder – 1 teaspoon
- Paprika – 1 teaspoon
- Salt – 1 teaspoon
- Black pepper – ½ teaspoon
- Cayenne pepper – ¼ teaspoon

## THE SMOKE

- Preheat your smoker to 250°F (121°C)
- Apple or pecan wood pellets work well with this recipe

## METHOD

1. In a bowl, using clean hands, combine the turkey with the green onions, breadcrumbs, barbecue sauce, ground oregano, garlic powder, paprika, salt, black pepper, and cayenne pepper.
2. Shape the mixture into 4-6 patties and slightly flatten.
3. Arrange the patties in a single layer on the smoker racks and smoke until their internal temperature registers 165°F (74°C).
4. Serve the burgers in buns and enjoy.

# Chapter-3 Lamb

## Lamb Burgers with Cheese

**(TOTAL COOK TIME 1 HOUR 15 MINUTES)**

**INGREDIENTS FOR 4-6 SERVINGS**

## THE MEAT

- Ground lamb (2-lbs, 0.9-kgs)

## THE INGREDIENTS

- Sea salt
- Freshly cracked black pepper
- Slices of Cheddar, American or Provolone
- Rolls, split, to serve

## THE SMOKE

- First, remove two of the smoker racks
- Preheat your smoker to 225°F (107°C) and open the top vent
- Add water to the water bowl
- Use hickory wood chips

## METHOD

1. Form the ground meat into patties of approximately ½ -ins (1.25-cms) thick.
2. Place the lamb patties on the smoker racks and liberally season on both sides with sea salt and cracked black pepper.
3. Arrange the racks on the smoker and smoke for between 1–1½ hours until they register an internal temperature of 160°F (71°C). Check the burgers smoking process after 1 hour. You may need to add additional wood chips or water at this stage.
4. When there is only 10-15 minutes of smoking remaining, place the slices of cheese on top of the burgers, and smoke for a few minutes, until entirely melted.
5. Place each burger in a bun along with your chosen toppings.

# LAMB CHOPS WITH GARLIC & HERBS

**(TOTAL COOK TIME 8 HOURS 35 MINUTES)**

## INGREDIENTS FOR 8 SERVINGS

### THE MEAT

- Lamb rib chops (4-lb, 1.8-kgs)

### THE RUB

- Fresh sage (16-ozs, 454-gms)
- 4 cloves of garlic, peeled
- 8 sprigs thyme
- Olive oil – 12 tablespoons
- Salt and freshly ground black pepper
- Butter

### THE SMOKE

- When you are ready to being cooking, preheat the smoker to 300°F (149°C)
- Place a cast iron skillet on the grates to heat

## METHOD

1. Using your fingers crush and pulverize the sage to release its fragrant oils.
2. In a bowl, combine the crushed sage with the garlic, and thyme.
3. Place the lamb chops on top of the herb mixture.
4. Drizzle oil over the lamb and liberally season with salt and black pepper. Toss, to evenly combine.
5. Cover the bowl with kitchen wrap and place in the fridge overnight, to chill.
6. The following day, remove the lamb chops from the bowl and arrange in the hot skillet along with a knob of butter. Baste the chops with the melted butter while cooking. The lamb is ready when it registers 120°F (49°C) on an internal meat thermometer.
7. Remove from the smoker, tent with aluminum foil and allow to rest for 5-6 minutes, before serving.

# *LAMB JERKY*

## (TOTAL COOK TIME 12 HOURS 15 MINUTES)

## INGREDIENTS FOR 4 SERVINGS

## THE MEAT

- Lamb , cut against the grain into ½ -ins (0.64-cms) thick strips, fat removed (1-lb, 0.45-kgs)

## THE MARINADE

- Soy sauce – ½ cup
- Worcestershire sauce – 2 tablespoons
- Runny honey – 2 tablespoons
- Red pepper flakes – 1 tablespoon
- Onion powder – 2 teaspoons
- Garlic powder – 2 teaspoons
- Black pepper – 1 teaspoon

## THE SMOKE

- Preheat your smoker grill to 165°F (74°C)
- Fill the water pan with water and add the wood chips
- Combine cherry wood with hickory wood chips. The combination will balance out the flavors.

## METHOD

1. Add the lamb, soy sauce, Worcestershire sauce, honey, red pepper flakes, onion powder, garlic powder and black pepper in a ziplock bag. Transfer to the fridge, overnight.
2. Remove the meat from the marinade, shaking off any excess.
3. Lay the meat flat on multiple racks. It is important that the strips are in a single layer and not overlapping.
4. Smoke for between 4-6 hours, until the meat, is firm and crisp.
5. Enjoy.

# SEASONED LEG OF LAM

## (TOTAL COOK TIME 12 HOURS 45 MINUTES)

## INGREDIENTS FOR 12-16 SERVINGS

## THE MEAT

- 1 bone-in, leg of lamb (8-lb, 3.62-kgs)

## THE SEASONING

- 9 small cloves of garlic, peeled
- Fresh oregano – 1 teaspoon
- 2 rosemary sprigs, needles stripped, stemmed
- Freshly squeezed juice of 2 medium-size lemons
- Extra-virgin olive oil – 6 tablespoons
- Sea salt and freshly ground black pepper

## THE SMOKE

- When you are ready to begin cooking, and with the lid open, start the grill on smoke and establish the fire, 4- 6 minutes
- Set the temperature to 400°F (205°C) and with the lid closed, preheat for 12-15 minutes
- Hickory wood pellets are a good choice for this recipe

# METHOD

1. With a paring knife, make a number of small-size slits in the lamb.
2. On a cutting board, finely mince the garlic, oregano, and sprigs of rosemary until a paste-like consistency.
3. Stuff a small amount of the paste into the slits. The best way to do this is to push the mixture into the slits using the back of a metal teaspoon.
4. Arrange the lamb leg on a rack, set inside a foil-lined roasting or baking tin.
5. Rub the surface of the lamb all over with the lemon juice and olive oil.
6. Cover entirely with kitchen wrap and place in the refrigerator, overnight.
7. The next day, take the lamb out of the fridge and put aside to come to room temperature.
8. Remove the kitchen wrap from the lamb and season with sea salt and freshly ground black pepper.
9. Roast the lamb on the preheated grill for 30 minutes, before turning the heat down to 350°F (177°C). Continue to cook until an internal thermometer inserted into the chunkiest part of the lamb, and not touching the bone, registers 145°F (63°C) for medium-rare or longer if your preference is for well-done. This will take around 3-4 hours.
10. Place the lamb on a cutting board and set to one side to rest for between 15-20 minutes before carving on the diagonal.
11. Serve and enjoy.

# SMOKED LAMB SAUSAGE WITH YOGURT SAUCE

## (TOTAL COOK TIME 2 HOURS 10 MINUTES)

## INGREDIENTS FOR 6-8 SERVINGS

## THE MEAT

- Lamb shoulder, cut into 2-ins (5-cms) pieces (2-lb, 0.9-kgs)
- 1 hog casing 60-ins (152-cms)

## THE SEASONING

- Garlic – 1 tablespoon
- Cumin – 1 teaspoon
- Paprika – 1 teaspoon
- Cayenne – ½ teaspoon
- Ground fennel – 2 tablespoons
- Cilantro, finely chopped – 1 tablespoon
- Parsley, finely chopped – 1 tablespoon
- Black pepper – 1 teaspoon
- Salt – 2 tablespoons

## THE SAUCE

- Greek yogurt – 3 cups
- Freshly squeezed juice of 1 lemon
- 1 garlic clove, peeled
- 1 cucumber, peeled, shredded, and drained
- Dill – 1 tablespoon
- Salt and black pepper

## THE GRILL

- When you are ready to begin cooking, preheat your grill to smoke and with the lid open establish the fire, for 4-6 minutes
- Preheat to 225°F (107°C).

## METHOD

1. First, using a meat grinder, grind the lamb.
2. In a bowl lightly combine the lamb with the garlic, cumin, paprika, cayenne, ground fennel, cilantro, parsley, black pepper, and salt. Transfer to the fridge; this will prevent the lamb fat from melting.
3. Next, with a sausage horn, attach the sausage casing and begin feeding the sausage back through the grinder to fill the casing, and twist into sausage links.
4. Using a paring knife, prick numerous holes along the sausage casing to allow any steam to escape during smoking. Cover and place in the fridge.
5. To prepare the sauce, combine the yogurt with the fresh lemon juice, garlic cloves, cucumber, dill, salt and black pepper in a bowl. Cover the bowl and place in the fridge until you are ready to use.
6. Arrange the sausage on the grill grate and smoke for 60 minutes.
7. When the hour has passed, remove the sausage from the grill.
8. Increase the temperature to 450°F (232°C) and preheat for between 12-15 minutes.
9. When the heat reaches the required temperature, return the sausage to the grill and cook for an additional 5 minutes. Flip over and continue to cook for another 5 minutes.
10. Server the sausage hot, with the yogurt sauce!

# Chapter-4 PORK

## BISCUITS & SMOKED SAUSAGE GRAVY

(TOTAL COOK TIME 1 HOUR 25 MINUTES)

**INGREDIENTS FOR 2-4 SERVINGS**

## THE MEAT

- Tube pork sausage, casings removed (12-ozs, 28-gms)

## THE BISCUITS

- All-purpose flour – 2 cups
- Baking powder – 3 teaspoons
- Salt – ½ teaspoons
- Butter, cold, cut into cubes – ½ cup
- Milk – ¾ cup

## THE GRAVY

- All-purpose flour – 2 tablespoons
- Milk – 2 cups
- Freshly ground black pepper

## THE SMOKE

- When you are ready to beginning cooking, set your grill to smoke and with the lid open establish the fire, 4-6 minutes

# METHOD

1. Place the unwrapped sausage roll directly on the grill grate, and smoke for between 30-60 minutes.
2. To prepare the biscuits: In a mixing bowl, whisk the flour with the baking powder and salt. Using a fork or pastry cutter, cut in the butter until the mixture is the consistency of breadcrumbs.
3. Stir in the milk to create a firm dough. You may need to add additional milk if needed, but take care not to over-mix.
4. Tip the dough onto a lightly floured work surface and with floured hands, gently knead until it comes together.
5. Pat the dough into a disk of approximately ½ -ins (1.25-cms). Cut the dough into round cookie shapes. Transfer to a parchment-lined ungreased baking sheet.
6. Once the sausage has smoked, remove it from the smoker and reduce the temperature of the grill to 450°F (232°C), and with the lid closed preheat for between 12-15 minutes.
7. While the biscuits bake, over moderately high heat, heat a large skillet.
8. Add the sausage to the skillet, and cook until well browned and sufficiently cooked through for approximately 7 minutes.
9. Using a slotted spoon, transfer the sausage to a mixing bowl, leaving any rendered fat remaining in the skillet.
10. Whisk the flour into the sausage fat and cook, while stirring for 60 seconds.
11. While you are whisking, pour the milk into the skillet and bring to boil.

12. Reduce the heat and gently simmer for 2 minutes.
13. Stir in the sausage and liberally season with black pepper.
14. Split the warm biscuits in half and place them on individual plates.
15. Top with gravy and enjoy.

# *JALAPENO CHEDDAR SMOKED SAUSAGE*

## (TOTAL COOK TIME 11 HOURS 20 MINUTES)

**INGREDIENTS FOR 6-8 SERVINGS**

## THE MEAT

- Ground pork (2-lbs, 0.9-kgs)
- 5 jalapenos, seeded, cut into small dice
- Mature cheddar, shredded – ½ cup
- Kosher salt – ½ tablespoon
- Freshly ground black pepper – 1 teaspoon
- Granulated garlic – 1 teaspoon
- Onion powder – 1 teaspoon

## THE SPECIAL EQUIPMENT

- Hog casings
- Sausage stuffer

## THE SMOKE

- When you are ready to beginning cooking, set the temperature to 180°F (82°C) and with the lid closed, preheat for 15 minutes
- Oak pellets are a good choice for this recipe

## METHOD

1. Place the hog casings in water and soak as per the package instructions.
2. In the meantime, while the casings soak, prepare the sausage.
3. Add the jalapenos, cheese, salt, pepper, garlic and onion powder to a food blender and on pulse, combine. Do not over-mix the mixture; it should be slightly tacky and fully incorporated.
4. Add the sausage mixture to your sausage stuff and stuff the casing according to the manufacturer's instructions. While it is important to stuff the length of the casing but also do not overstuff as this may cause the casing to burst when you prepare the links.
5. Hang the sausages at room temperature for 60 minutes, to dry, before transferring to the fridge overnight.
6. When you are ready to cook, prepare your smoker as directed above.
7. Arrange the sausage directly on the grill grate and smoke for between 2-3 hours, until they reach an internal temperature of 155°F (68°C).
8. Serve and enjoy.

# PORK BUTT SANDWICH

## (TOTAL COOK TIME 8 HOURS 30 MINUTES)

## INGREDIENTS FOR 6-8 SERVINGS

## THE MEAT

- Boston butt pork roast, bone-in, fat trimmed, rinsed and patted dry (4-lbs, 1.8-kgs)
- Bread buns, of choice, split

## THE RUB

- Kosher salt – ¼ cup
- Firmly packed dark brown sugar – ¼ cup
- Smoked paprika – 2 tablespoons + 2 teaspoons
- Granulated sugar – 2 tablespoons
- Garlic powder – 2 teaspoons
- Freshly ground black pepper – 2 tablespoons
- Dry mustard – 1 teaspoon
- Ground ginger – 1 teaspoon
- Ground cumin – 1 teaspoon

## THE TOPPINGS

- BBQ sauce, any brand
- Coleslaw, store-bought
- Dill pickles

## THE SMOKE

- When you are ready to begin cooking bring the smoker temperature to 250°F (121°C)

## METHOD

1. For the sauce, combine all the rub ingredients (salt, brown sugar, paprika, sugar, garlic powder, pepper, mustard, ginger, and cumin). Sprinkle over the pork and set aside to stand for half an hour at room temperature.
2. Place the pork, fatty side facing upwards on the grate in the middle of the smoker and directly over the coals.
3. Cover the smoker with lid and make adjustments to the ventilation to ensure the temperature is constant and smoke for 5 hours.
4. Turn the pork over, fatty side facing down and smoke for an additional 2-3 hours, or until the meat registers 195°F (90°C) on an internal meat thermometer.
5. Transfer to a chopping board, and allow to cool for 15 minutes and shred the meat.
6. Assemble the sandwich on the bread buns along with your choice of BBQ sauce, slaw, and pickles.
7. Serve and enjoy.

# *SMOKED APPLEWOOD BACON*

## (TOTAL COOK TIME 8 DAYS 3 HOURS)

## INGREDIENTS FOR 8-10 SERVINGS

### THE MEAT

- Pork belly, skinned (2-lbs, 0.9-kgs)

## THE CURE

- Sea salt – ½ cup
- Brown sugar – ½ cup
- Crushed black pepper – 1 tablespoon

## THE SMOKE

- When you are ready to beginning cooking, set your grill to smoke and with the lid closed preheat to 180°F (82°C)
- For the bacon: When you are ready to cook start the grill and set to 400°F (204°C) and with the lid closed preheat for between 12-15 minutes

## METHOD

1. In a bowl, combine the cure ingredients: salt, brown sugar, and black pepper.
2. Pour the cure over the pork belly.
3. Add the pork and the cure to a large ziplock bag. Expel as much air from the bag as is possible. Transfer to the fridge for 8 days.
4. Every 48 hours, turn the pork belly over. It is very important that the juice covers both sides of the pork to ensure an even cure.
5. When 8 days have elapsed remove the pork from the refrigerator and rinse thoroughly under cold running water. Using kitchen paper towels, pat dry.
6. Add a layer of ice to a jelly roll pan.

7. Arrange a rack on top of the ice.
8. Place the pork belly on top of the rack.
9. Place the pan of ice, rack, and pork directly onto the grill grate.
10. Smoke the pork belly for between 2-3 hours, until it reaches an internal temperature of 150°F (65°C).
11. Once the smoke is smoked, wrap in kitchen wrap, before placing in the freezer for between 30-60 minutes, or until the bacon is virtually frozen.
12. Slice the bacon to your preferred thickness.
13. When you are ready to cook the bacon: Arrange the slices of bacon directly on the grill grate at 400°F (204°C) and cook, flipping over once or twice until your preferred crispness, for between 8-10 minutes.
14. Remove the bacon to a kitchen paper-towel-lined plate.
15. Serve and enjoy.

# ST LOUIS RIBS WITH COCONUT BBQ RIB SAUCE

(TOTAL COOK TIME 6 HOURS 20 MINUTES)

**INGREDIENTS FOR 8-12 SERVINGS**

## THE MEAT

- 3 racks St. Louis style ribs, trimmed with membrane removed

## THE SAUCE

- BBQ sauce, of choice – 2 cups
- Rum – 2 cups
- Coconut milk – 3½ cups
- 2 tomatoes, chopped
- 2 cloves roasted garlic, peeled, and chopped

## THE SEASONING

- Garlic and chili pepper rub, any brand – 4 tablespoons
- Butter – 6 tablespoons
- Brown sugar – 1½ cups
- Agave – 1½ cups

## THE SMOKE

- When you are ready to beginning cooking, set your grill to 350°F (177°C) and with the lid closed, preheat for between 12-15 minutes
- Applewood chips are recommended for this recipe

## METHOD

1. First, prepare the sauce: Add the BBQ sauce, rum, coconut milk, tomatoes, and garlic to a pan, stirring to combine entirely.
2. Transfer the pan to the grill grate and cook for 45-60 minutes.
3. Remove the pan from the grate and transfer the mixture to a food blender; puree until silky smooth. Set to one side.
4. For the ribs: Turn the grill temperature to 250°F (121°C).
5. Season the ribs with the rub and arrange them directly on the grate rib side facing down, cook for 3 hours.
6. Place two sheets of aluminum foil on a table. In the middle of the foil, place 3 tablespoons of butter, ½ cup of brown sugar and the agave.
7. Arrange the ribs, meat side facing downwards on top of the mixture and tightly wrap. Repeat the process with the remaining racks.
8. Place all the racks directly on the grill grate, meat side facing downwards and cook for another 1½-2hours, or until the meat registers 203°F (95°F).
9. Remove the rib racks from the grill and cover each one with a ½ cup of the coconut rum BBQ sauce. Re-wrap the racks and return to the grill for 10 minutes; this will allow the sauce to thicken.
10. Take the ribs off the grill, slice, and serve.

# Chapter-5 Fish

## Fennel & Pepper Stuffed Smoked Trout

**(TOTAL COOK TIME 45 MINUTES)**

**INGREDIENTS FOR 4 SERVINGS**

## THE FISH

- 4 whole trout, boned, intestines removed, prepared for stuffing

## THE INGREDIENTS

- Salt – 2 teaspoons
- Freshly cracked black pepper – 2 teaspoons
- 6-8 small sweet peppers, sliced
- 1 fennel plant, sliced
- Butter, cut into 1 tablespoon slices – ½ cup
- Olive oil – 2 tablespoons

## THE SMOKE

- Preheat your smoker grill to 250°F (121°C)

## METHOD

1. Sprinkle salt and black pepper over the sweet peppers and fennel.
2. Arrange the trout on a baking sheet.
3. Fill the fish cavity from head to tail with the peppers and fennel.
4. Add 1 tablespoon of butter to each cavity.
5. Lay the fish on the grill and smoke for between 30-45 minutes, until the fish registers an internal temperature of 145°F (63°C).
6. Drizzle with oil and serve.

# HERB SMOKED SALMON

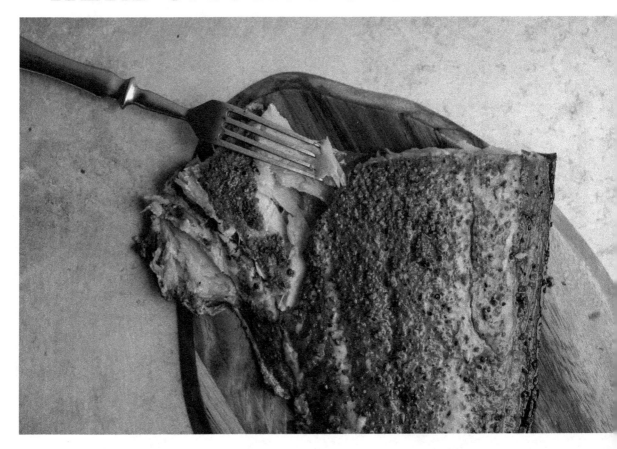

(TOTAL COOK TIME 1 HOUR 5 MINUTES)

**INGREDIENTS FOR 4 SERVINGS**

## THE FISH

- 4 salmon fillets
- Freshly squeezed juice of a ¼ lemon
- Olive oil – 1 tablespoon

## THE SEASONING

- Fresh dill, minced – 1 teaspoon
- Celery seed – ¼ teaspoon
- Paprika – ½ teaspoons
- Salt – 1 teaspoon
- Freshly ground black pepper – ½ teaspoon

## THE CRÈME FRAICHE

- Crème Fraiche – ½ cup
- Zest of ½ a fresh lemon
- Freshly squeezed juice of a ¼ lemon
- Shallot, minced – 1 tablespoon
- Fresh tarragon, minced – 2 tablespoons

## THE SMOKE

- Preheat your smoker grill to 285°F (140°C)

## METHOD

1. In a bowl, combine the fresh lemon juice with the oil, whisk and lightly brush over the salmon.
2. In a second bowl, combine the dill with the celery seeds, paprika, salt, and black pepper. Sprinkle over the fish.
3. Arrange the fish on the grill grates and smoke for 60 minutes.
4. For the crème Fraiche: In a bowl, combine the crème Fraiche with the lemon zest, fresh lemon juice, shallots, and tarragon. Cover the bowl, and place in the fridge, to chill.
5. Serve the salmon with the crème fraiche and garnish with a slice of lemon.

# SESAME CRUSTED SMOKED HALIBUT WITH TAHINI MAYO

(TOTAL COOK TIME 2 HOURS 30 MINUTES)

**INGREDIENTS FOR 4 SERVINGS**

## THE FISH

- Halibut fillet (1½ -lbs, 0.68-kgs)

## THE INGREDIENTS

- Toasted sesame seeds – ½ cup
- Sea salt flakes – ½ teaspoon
- Vegetable oil – 1 tablespoon
- Sesame oil – 1 teaspoon

## THE MAYONNAISE

- 2 egg yolks
- Freshly squeezed lemon juice – 2 tablespoons
- Tahini paste – ¼ cup
- Soy sauce – 1 tablespoon
- Vegetable oil – 1 ½ cups

## THE SMOKE

- Preheat your smoker grill to 225°F (107°C)
- Pecan or cherry wood pellets are a good choice for this recipe

# METHOD

2. Using a pestle and mortar, crush the sesame seeds together with the salt, until gently crushed rather than a powder.
3. In a bowl, blend the vegetable and sesame oil together, and brush all over the fish.
4. Coat each portion of fish with the seasoned sesame seeds, gently patting them all over the surface of the halibut.
5. Arrange the fish on the lower rack of your pellet grill and close its lid.
6. Transfer the fish to the smoker for 2- 2½ hours or until it reaches an internal temperature of 145°F (63°C).
7. To prepare the homemade mayonnaise: In a food blender, combine the egg yolks with the lemon juice, tahini paste, and soy sauce. On high, very slowly and in a steady stream, add the vegetable oil. As you drizzle in the oil, it will emulsify to create a thick creamy mayonnaise.
8. Serve the halibut along with the tahini mayonnaise, and enjoy.

# Chapter-6 SEAFOOD

# HICKORY SMOKED CAJUN SHRIMP

(TOTAL COOK TIME 4 HOURS 30 MINUTES)

## INGREDIENTS FOR 4-6 SERVINGS

## THE SEAFOOD

- Raw shrimp, peeled, deveined (2-lbs, 0.9-kgs)

## THE MARINADE

- Cajun seasoning shake – 1 tablespoon
- Freshly squeezed juice of 1 lemon
- 2 cloves of garlic, peeled, minced
- Extra-virgin olive oil – 4 tablespoons
- Sea salt – 1 teaspoon

## THE SMOKE

- Preheat the grill on smoke and establish the fire, for 4-6 minutes
- Close the smoker lid and increase the temperature to high, allowing the grill to preheat for 12-15 minutes
- Hickory wood pellets are recommended for this recipe

## METHOD

1. Prepare the marinade: In a ziplock bag, combine the Cajun shake seasoning with the fresh lemon juice, garlic cloves, oil and sea salt.
2. Add the shrimp to the bag and toss gently to evenly coat.
3. Allow the shrimp to marinate, covered for 3-4 hours.
4. Remove the shrimp from the bag, shaking off and discarding any marinade.
5. Thread the shrimp onto skewers and place directly on the smoker grill, cooking until opaque, for 3-4 minutes each side.

# *LITTLENECK SMOKED CLAMS*

**(TOTAL COOK TIME 30 MINUTES)**

## INGREDIENTS FOR 4-6 SERVINGS

## THE SEAFOOD

- Littleneck clams, scrubbed, rinsed, and shucked (2-lbs, 0.9-kgs)

## THE INGREDIENTS

- Lemon wedges
- Fresh parsley, minced
- Marie rose cocktail sauce, any brand

## THE SMOKE

- Preheat the smoker for 225°F (107°c)
- Applewood or maple wood pellets are recommended for this recipe

## METHOD

1. Arrange the shucked clams on a vegetable grate and smoke for between 30-40 minutes.
2. Garnish with parsley and serve with Marie Rose sauce, enjoy.

# PAPRIKA & GARLIC BUTTER SMOKED LOBSTER TAILS

**(TOTAL COOK TIME 1 HOUR 10 MINUTES)**

**INGREDIENTS FOR 2 SERVINGS**

## THE SEAFOOD

- 2 lobster tails (10-ozs, 283-gms) each

## THE INGREDIENTS

- Butter – 4 tablespoons
- Freshly squeezed lemon juice – 2 tablespoons
- Smoked paprika – 1 teaspoon
- Garlic, peeled, chopped – ¼ teaspoon
- Old Bay seasoning - ½ teaspoon
- Garlic salt  ½ teaspoon
- Fresh parsley, chopped, optional – 2 tablespoons

## THE SMOKE

- Prepare your smoker to 225°F (107°C)
- Add your favorite flavor wood pellets

## METHOD

1. First, prepare the lobster tail by cutting a slit from the top of the shell to the tail.
2. In a microwave-safe bowl, combine the butter with the fresh lemon juice, smoked paprika, garlic, Old Bay seasoning, and garlic salt.
3. Place the bowl in the microwave and on high heat, microwave for no more than 30 seconds, or until the butter is completely melted. Stir well to incorporate.
4. Arrange the tails on the preheated smoker with the slit side face upwards and with the butter-garlic salt mixture, baste every 15-20 minutes.
5. When approximately 45 minutes have elapsed, move the lobster tails closer to the heat, while still keeping the slit side face upwards.
6. Continue to smoke for a couple more minutes. This will ensure that the tails are sufficiently warmed through. Cooking times will depend on your make and model of smoker and the distance the lobster tails are from the heat. The lobster tails are ready to serve when they reach an internal temperature of 140°F (60°C).
7. Garnish with parsley and enjoy.

# Chapter-7 GAME

# BISON & BOAR SAUSAGES

**(TOTAL COOK TIME 13 HOURS 10 MINUTES)**

**INGREDIENTS FOR 4-6 SERVINGS**

## THE GAME

- Ground wild bison (8-oz, 227-gms)
- Ground wild boar (8-oz, 227-gms)

## THE INGREDIENTS

- Fast cure salt mix – 1½ teaspoons
- Kosher salt – 1 tablespoon
- Mustard seeds – ½ teaspoon
- Black pepper – ½ teaspoon
- Garlic powder – ½ teaspoon
- Fresh thyme leaves – ½ tablespoon

## THE SMOKE

- Preheat the smoker with the lid closed for 15 minutes, to 225°F (107°C)

## METHOD

1. In a bowl, combine all of the ingredients (ground bison, ground wild boar, fast cure salt mix, kosher salt, mustard seeds, black pepper, garlic powder, and thyme leaves). Be careful not to over-mix and set to one side, overnight.
2. Form the mixture into a log shape and wrap in kitchen wrap. Twist the ends of the wrap tightly and smooth out the log using clean hands.
3. Slowly unwrap to retain the shape and place directly on the grill grate, smoking for between 3-4 hours.
4. Remove and set aside to cool for 60 minutes.
5. When sufficiently cool, wrap and transfer to the fridge until ready to serve.

# DUCK LEGS WITH POLENTA & MUSHROOMS

## (TOTAL COOK TIME 13 HOURS)

## INGREDIENTS FOR 4-6 SERVINGS

## THE GAME

- 6 duck legs

## THE MARINADE

- Kosher salt – ¼ cup
- 4 garlic cloves, peeled and ground to a paste
- Thyme, chopped – 1 tablespoon
- Shallot, chopped – 1 tablespoon
- 1 bay leaf, crushed
- Zest of 1 fresh lemon
- Zest of 1 fresh orange

## THE POLENTA

- Chicken stock, divided – 5½ cups
- Coarsely ground polenta – 1 cup
- Kosher salt, to taste
- Unsalted butter, divided – 4 tablespoons
- Wild mushrooms, sliced – 3 cups
- Salt and black pepper
- Fresh thyme leaves – ½ tablespoon

## THE SMOKE

- When you are ready to beginning cooking, start your smoker grill on smoke, with the lid open and establish a fire, for 4-6 minutes
- Preheat, with the lid closed to 180°F (82°C) for 12-15 minutes
- Mesquite wood pellets are recommended for this recipe

## METHOD

1. In a bowl, combine the salt with the garlic paste, thyme, shallot, bay leaf, lemon zest, and orange zest.
2. Cover the duck legs with the salt-citrus zest mixture and place in the fridge, overnight.
3. Remove the duck from the mixture, rinse until cold water, and using kitchen paper towels and pat dry.
4. Arrange the duck legs on the grill grate and smoke until the meat is easy to shred; this will take between 4-5 hours.
5. For the polenta: Over moderate-high heat, in a pan, bring 5 cups of chicken stock to boil.
6. Once boiling has been achieved, pour in the polenta, while whisking until lump-free.
7. Turn the heat down to simmer and cook until the polenta is al dente.
8. Should the polenta appear too dry add a drop of water.
9. Season with salt and stir in 2 tablespoons butter. Keep the polenta warm.
10. Next, prepare the mushrooms. Over high heat in a pan, melt the remaining butter.

11. Add the mushrooms to the pan and cook until gently browned and a little crisp.
12. Pour in the chicken stock and season with salt and pepper.
13. Transfer to the grill at 350°F (177°F) and while the duck rests cook for between 20-30 minutes. Sprinkle with thyme.
14. When you are ready to serve, spoon the polenta into a serving dish. Top with the mushrooms and duck legs.
15. Season with sea salt and serve.

# *SMOKED BBQ RABBIT*

**(TOTAL COOK TIME 4 HOURS 15 MINUTES)**

**INGREDIENTS FOR 4 SERVINGS**

## THE GAME

- 1 cottontail rabbit, skinned and gutted

## THE BRINE

- Kosher salt – 2 tablespoons
- White wine vinegar – ½ cup

## THE RUB

- Cayenne pepper – 1 tablespoon
- Garlic powder – 1 tablespoon
- Salt – 1 tablespoon
- Freshly ground black pepper – 1 tablespoon
- Barbecue sauce, of choice

## THE SMOKE

- Preheat your smoker grill to 225°F (107°C)
- Hickory or mesquite wood pellets are recommended for this recipe

# METHOD

1. For the brine, dissolve the salt in the white wine vinegar.
2. Add the rabbit to a shallow dish.
3. Pour the brine over the rabbit along with sufficient water, to cover. Set aside for 60 minutes.
4. Remove the rabbit from the brine and using kitchen paper towels, pat dry.
5. In a bowl, whisk equal parts of cayenne pepper, garlic powder, salt, and black pepper, and heavily season the rabbit with the rub.
6. Transfer the rabbit to the smoker.
7. After 15 minutes have elapsed mop the rabbit with the BBQ sauce, repeating the process every 15 minutes.
8. The rabbit is sufficiently cooked when it registers an internal temperature of at least 160°F (71°C). This will take around 3 hours.

# Chapter-8 Vegetables

# Cajun Artichokes

### (TOTAL COOK TIME 2 HOURS)

## INGREDIENTS FOR 4 SERVINGS

## THE VEGETABLES

- 1 2-16 canned, whole artichoke hearts

## THE SEASONING

- Cajun seasoning – 2 tablespoons

## THE SMOKE

- Preheat the smoker, for cold smoking
- Hickory wood pellets are recommended for this recipe

## METHOD

1. Slice the artichoke hearts in half.
2. Toss the artichoke halves in the Cajun seasoning.
3. Spread the hearts in a single layer on the smoker rack and cold smoke for 2 hours.
4. Serve and enjoy.

# SMOKED OLIVES

## (TOTAL COOK TIME 1 HOUR)

## INGREDIENTS FOR 6-8 SERVINGS

## THE VEGETABLES

- Kalamata olives, pitted, drained – 1 cup
- Green olives, drained – 1 cup

## THE INGREDIENTS

- Extra-virgin olive oil – 2 tablespoons
- White wine – 2 tablespoons
- 2 cloves of garlic, peeled, and minced
- Dried rosemary – ¾ teaspoon
- Freshly ground black pepper
- Asiago cheese, freshly grated, to serve, optional

## THE SMOKE

- Preheat the pellet grill to 220°F (104°C)

## METHOD

1. Arrange the olives on a sheet of heavy aluminum foil molded into a small foil tray.
2. Add the olive oil, white wine, garlic, dried rosemary, and black pepper. Toss to coat evenly.
3. Transfer the olives to the smoker and cook for between 30-50 minutes, until smoky in flavor. It is recommended to check the smoking process after 20 minutes.
4. Serve with the grated cheese and enjoy.

# SMOKED VEGGIE MEDLEY

**(TOTAL COOK TIME 1 HOUR)**

## INGREDIENTS FOR 4 SERVINGS

## THE VEGETABLES

- 1 Spanish red onion, peeled and cut into quarters
- 1 red pepper, seeded and sliced
- 2 zucchinis, sliced
- 1 yellow summer squash, sliced

## THE INGREDIENTS

- Olive oil – 2 tablespoons
- Balsamic vinegar – 2 tablespoons
- 6 garlic cloves, peeled, minced
- Sea salt – 1 teaspoon
- Black pepper – ½ teaspoon

## THE SMOKE

- Preheat the pellet grill to 350°F (177°C)
- Hickory or mesquite wood pellets are recommended for this recipe

## METHOD

1. In a large bowl, combine the red onion, red pepper, zucchinis, summer squash, olive oil, balsamic vinegar, garlic, sea salt, and black pepper. Toss to combine.
2. Transfer the veggies to the smoker and with the lid closed cook for between 30-45 minutes, until cooked through and caramelized.
3. Serve and enjoy.

# Chapter-9 Smoking Tips and Tricks

## Difference Between Barbequing and Smoking

You might not believe it, but there are still people who think that the process of Barbequing and Smoking are the same! So, this is something which you should know about before diving in deeper.

So, whenever you are going to use a traditional BBQ grill, you always put your meat directly on top of the heat source for a brief amount of time which eventually cooks up the meal. Smoking, on the other hand, will require you to combine the heat from your grill as well as the smoke to infuse a delicious smoky texture and flavor to your meat. Smoking usually takes much longer than traditional barbecuing. In most cases, it takes a minimum of 2 hours and a temperature of 100 -120 degrees for the smoke to be properly infused into the meat. Keep in mind that the time and temperature will obviously depend on the type of meat that you are using, and that is why it is suggested that you keep a meat thermometer handy to ensure that your meat is doing fine. Keep in mind that this method of barbecuing is also known as "Low and slow" smoking as well. With that cleared up, you should be aware that there are actually two different ways through which smoking is done.

# Difference Between Cold and Hot Smoking

Depending on the type of grill that you are using, you might be able to get the option to go for a Hot Smoking Method or a Cold Smoking One. The primary fact about these three different cooking techniques which you should keep in mind are as follows:

- **Hot Smoking:** In this technique, the food will use both the heat on your grill and the smoke to prepare your food. This method is most suitable for items such as chicken, lamb, brisket etc.
- **Cold Smoking:** In this method, you are going to smoke your meat at a very low temperature such as 30 degree Celsius, making sure that it doesn't come into the direct contact with the heat. This is mostly used as a means to preserve meat and extend their life on the shelf.
- **Roasting Smoke:** This is also known as Smoke Baking. This process is essentially a combined form of both roasting and baking and can be performed in any type of smoker with a capacity of reaching temperatures above 82 degree Celsius.

By now you must be really curious to know about the different types of Smokers that are out there right?

Well, in the next section I am exactly going to discuss that!

# *Basic Preparations*

- Always be prepared to spend the whole day and take as much time as possible to smoke your meat for maximum effect.
- Make sure to obtain the perfect Ribs/Meat for the meal which you are trying to smoke. Do a little bit of research if you need.
- I have already added a list of woods in this book, consult to that list and choose the perfect wood for your meal.
- Make sure to prepare the marinade for each of the meals properly. A great deal of the flavor comes from the rubbing.
- Keep a meat thermometer handy to get the internal temperature when needed.
- Use mittens or tongs to keep yourself safe
- Refrain yourself from using charcoal infused alongside starter fluid as it might bring a very unpleasant odor to your food
- Always make sure to start off with a small amount of wood and keep adding them as you cook.
- Don't be afraid to experiment with different types of wood for newer flavor and experiences.
- Always keep a notebook near you and note jot down whatever you are doing or learning and use them during the future session. This will help you to evolve and move forward.

# Elements of Smoking

Smoking is a very indirect method of cooking that relies on a number of different factors to give you the most perfectly cooked meal that you are looking for. Each of these components is very important to the whole process as they all work together to create the meal of your dreams.

- **Time**: Unlike grilling or even Barbequing, smoking takes a really long time and requires a whole lot of patience. It takes time for the smoky flavor to slowly get infused into the meats. Jus to bring things into comparison, it takes an about 8 minutes to fully cook a steak through direct heating, while smoking (indirect heating) will take around 35-40 minutes.
- **Temperature:** When it comes to smoking, the temperature is affected by a lot of different factors that are not only limited to the wind, cold air temperatures but also the cooking wood's dryness. Some smokers work best with large fires that are controlled by the draw of a chimney and restricted airflow through the various vents of the cooking chamber and firebox. While other smokers tend to require smaller fire with fewer coals as well as a completely different combination of the vent and draw controls. However, most smokers are designed to work at temperatures as low as 180 degrees Fahrenheit to as high as 300 degrees Fahrenheit. But the recommend temperature usually falls between 250 degrees Fahrenheit and 275 degrees Fahrenheit.
- **Airflow:** The level of air to which the fire is exposed to greatly determines how your fire will burn and how quickly it will burn the fuel. For instance, if you restrict air flow into the firebox by closing up the available vents, then the fire will burn at a low temperature and vice versa. Typically in smokers, after lighting up the fire, the vents are opened to allow for maximum air flow and is then adjusted throughout the cooking process to make sure that optimum flame is achieved.

**Insulation:** Insulation is also very important when it comes to smokers as it helps to easily manage the cooking process throughout the whole cooking session. A good insulation allows smokers to efficiently reach the desired temperature instead of waiting for hours upon hours!

# *Choose your wood*

You need to choose your wood carefully because the type of wood you will use affect greatly to the flavor and taste of the meat. Here are a few options for you:

- Maple: Maple has a smoky and sweet taste and goes well with pork or poultry

- Alder: Alder is sweet and light. Perfect for poultry and fish.

- Apple: Apple has a mild and sweet flavor. Goes well with pork, fish, and poultry.

- Oak: Oak is great for slow cooking. Ideal for game, pork, beef, and lamb.

- Mesquite: Mesquite has a smoky flavor and extremely strong. Goes well with pork or beef.

- Hickory: Has a smoky and strong flavor. Goes well with beef and lamb.

- Cherry Has a mild and sweet flavor. Great for pork, beef, and turkey

*To cook the meat, you may refer the below mentioned chart that can help you with selecting the best wood chips/chunks*

| Wood Type | Lamb | Chicken | Beef | Pork |
|---|---|---|---|---|
| Apple | Yes | Yes | No | No |
| Alder | Yes | Yes | No | Yes |
| Cherry | Yes | Yes | Yes | Yes |
| Hickory | No | No | Yes | Yes |
| Maple | No | Yes | No | No |
| Mulberry | Yes | Yes | No | Yes |
| Mesquite | No | No | Yes | Yes |
| Oak | Yes | Yes | Yes | Yes |
| Pecan | No | Yes | Yes | Yes |
| Pear | No | Yes | No | Yes |
| Peach | No | Yes | No | Yes |
| Walnut | No | No | Yes | Yes |

Remember, black smoke is bad and white smoke is good. Ensue proper ventilation for great tasting smoked meat.

# SELECT THE RIGHT MEAT

Some meats are just ideal for the smoking process, including:
- Chicken
- Turkey
- Pork roast
- Ham
- Brisket
- Pork and beef ribs
- Corned beef

# FIND THE RIGHT TEMPERATURE

- Start at 250F (120C): Start your smoker a bit hot. This extra heat gets the smoking process going.

- Temperature drop: Once you add the meat to the smoker, the temperature will drop, which is fine.

- Maintain the temperature. Monitor and maintain the temperature. Keep the temperature steady during the smoking process.

Avoid peeking every now and then. Smoke and heat two most important element makes your meat taste great. If you open the cover every now and then you lose both of them and your meat lose flavor. Only the lid only when you truly need it.

# CONCLUSION

I can't express how honored I am to think that you found my book interesting and informative enough to read it all through to the end. I thank you again for purchasing this book and I hope that you had as much fun reading it as I had writing it. I bid you farewell and encourage you to move forward and find your true Smoked Meat spirit!

# GET YOUR FREE GIFT

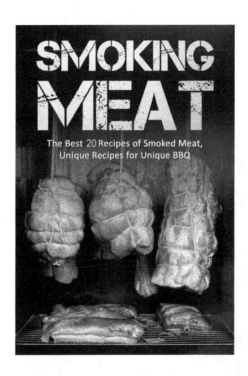

Subscribe to our Mail List and get your FREE copy of the book
'Smoking Meat: The Best 20 Recipes of Smoked Meat, Unique Recipes for Unique BBQ'

https://tiny.cc/smoke20

# Other books by Gary Mercer

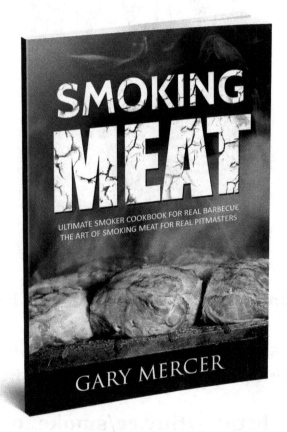

https://www.amazon.com/dp/1975935004

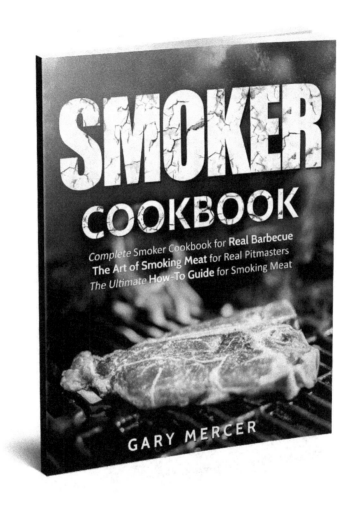

https://www.amazon.com/dp/1986445976

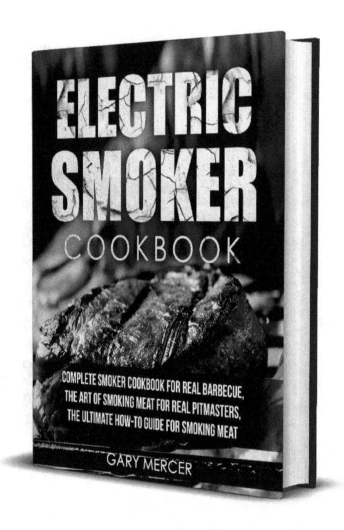

https://www.amazon.com/dp/1719264090

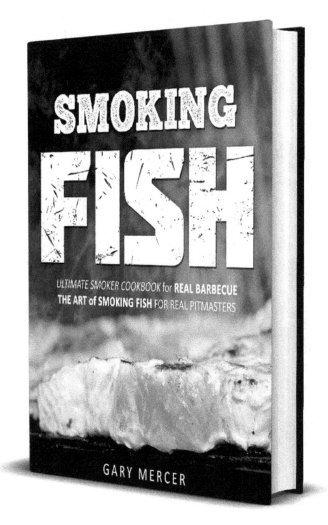

https://www.amazon.com/dp/1731585209

P.S. Thank you for reading this book. If you've enjoyed this book, please don't shy, drop me a line, leave a feedback or both on Amazon. I love reading feedbacks and your opinion is extremely important for me.

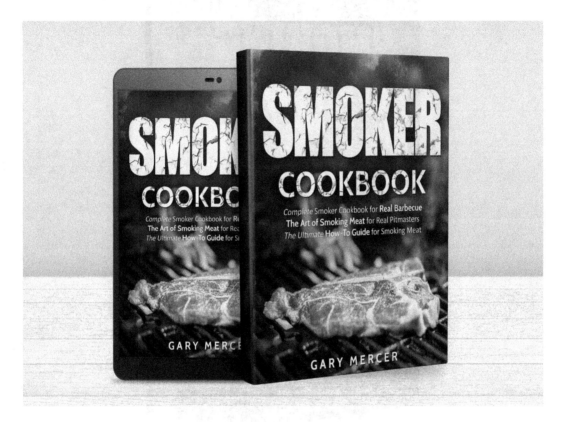

My Amazon page:

www.amazon.com/author/garymercer

©Copyright 2019 by **Gary Mercer** - All rights reserved.

All rights Reserved. No part of this publication or the information in it may be quoted from or reproduced in any form by means such as printing, scanning, photocopying or otherwise without prior written permission of the copyright holder.

***Disclaimer and Terms of Use:****The effort has been made to ensure that the information in this book is accurate and complete, however, the author and the publisher do not warrant the accuracy of the information, text, and graphics contained within the book due to the rapidly changing nature of science, research, known and unknown facts and the internet. The Author and the publisher do not hold any responsibility for errors, omissions or contrary interpretation of the subject matter herein. This book is presented solely for motivational and informational purposes only.*

CPSIA information can be obtained
at www.ICGtesting.com
Printed in the USA
LVHW101100141219
640498LV00020B/1581/P